ENGRAVERS

A HANDBOOK FOR THE NINETIES

ENGRAVERS

A HANDBOOK FOR THE NINETIES

Compiled for the Society of Wood Engravers
and with an introduction by

SIMON BRETT

SILENT BOOKS
1987

All engravings are reproduced actual size,
unless otherwise indicated.

Dedication
to Hilary Paynter

INTRODUCTION

The first purpose of this book is to put into permanent record a new generation of wood engravers, who have begun to work or to be noticed over the past ten years; the book is arranged chronologically beginning with these youngest. It aims, secondly, to present work by a full range of currently active engravers, to the public and to editors and art directors: their perception of engraving can be crucial and constructive. Thirdly, it seeks to affect that perception – of what engravings are about and thus of the uses to which they can be put.

As any artist will insist, subject matter is not the most important thing; but it is evident, too, that an art which deals only with limited areas of experience is in danger of becoming a minor art. The present revival of interest in the practice of wood engraving is pushing it in new directions, technically and expressively. The parallel and welcome revival in its use by publishers and editors tends to confirm its more conventional face; despite the recognition and employment of artists such as Peter Forster and Edwina Ellis or the illustrations to *The Iron Man* commissioned from Andrew Davidson, you will usually find the wood engravings on the cookery and garden pages. It need not be so, as these pages demonstrate.

That is to say, it need not be exclusively so. The classic, rich, infinitely various response to the natural world which engraving seems so ideally suited to, a familiar imagery which by its familiarity allows the sensibility of each artist to appear, is also generously represented here. It is the vernacular of wood engraving and will probably remain so as long as the name of Bewick is remembered. Claire Dalby, Ian Stephens, Miriam Macgregor and Chris Wormell honour this tradition, in very different ways.

As a means of self-expression, engraving has been described, by Peter Forster, as 'just about as spontaneous as making a soufflé'. Few in any generation are drawn to its difficulties and so, though not necessarily a minor art, it always tends to be a minority one; of the engravers in this book, only a handful do it full-time, most (like most artists) have other jobs, and some would describe themselves as amateurs. It would be unrealistic and unfair to issue some challenge to expand engraving, to them all, regardless of their degree of commitment. Nevertheless, if the soufflé does not rise, it will fall. If only the line from Bewick is trod, only narrowly, it will peter out. If no one expands the range of experience with which an art form deals, that art will ossify or dwindle.

This challenge, which artists face continually (but which stands as an invitation to those who determine how they shall be employed) is being met today with a self-aware, eclectic expertise that is completely of the 1980s; and at the same time an older generation of engravers is at its peak, having arrived there almost unacknowledged under the long (and illustrious) shadow of the 1920s and '30s. Since many of that inter-war generation are still active too, engraving has seldom in this century been pursued by so many generations of artists, without being dominated by any one of them.

It stands at a familiar crossroads: between having been recently saved from extinction by, once again, graphic and illustrational applications, and never quite having achieved the independent life which the inter-war period seemed to promise it but which the Second World War interrupted; nothing could be resumed on the same scale after a war. To urge those with commissions to free artists from stereotyped subject-matter, and to point away from commissions towards the independent print, which does not earn them a living, are part of the same question: whether engraving may one day become a medium any artist – not just any graphic artist – might employ, as painting or sculpture are. History seems determined to cheat it of this ordinary heritage, as it is to short-circuit the influence of the few important twentieth century artists who have been attracted to the medium.

Almost as soon as wood engraving was invented it was exploited by the reproductive engravers of the nineteenth century to such an extent and with such formidable technique that all twentieth century practice has appeared as a series of reactions and revivals by comparison. The initial and major reaction was against the soul-destroying skill of the nineteenth century, in favour of direct artistic expression; and the revivals have been of Thomas Bewick's original 'white-line' approach, of boldness and in its turn of finesse, and of reproductive engraving techniques themselves though on a different scale. Above all, there are periodic lapses and revivals of interest in relief printmaking as such, as it appears to 'stand for' different values at different times; and, in particular, in relief print-making on a fine scale.

Size *is* definitive. The small size of the tools it is done with and the fine texture of the material it is done on – classically boxwood – determine the size of an engraving and the kind of visual attention it commands. An artist may 'obey' the small size or react against it, but beyond a certain size he inevitably commands a different sort of attention and finds himself making a different sort of print.

The word 'relief' is definitive; for the way the engraving is printed determines the nature of the image.

Though several of the engravings in this book were not done on wood but on synthetic materials and though they are not printed from blocks but photographically reproduced, the images can only be created in one way: by engraving a flat surface into relief and printing the result. That is why, however much the sequence of lapses and revivals may sometimes look like a long and dusty operatic death, there always seems to be another aria to be sung; and this, despite the smallness of the company. Fine relief engraving is now part of human language. Blast them with wars, starve them of teaching, people find their way back to it, and reinvent it for themselves if necessary.

When the odds are against, as they have been for twenty years, a hundred fashions in painting may come and go while a few scattered engravers struggle on in isolation. Sheer survival does not make the work good, does not make it flourish as more than a small and stubborn thing. When a revival occurs, as now, larger questions of quality arise. The answers are simple. The quality of engraving, what will make it strong and good now and in the future, depends on the quality of its practitioners as artists – artists in the full sense: artists who confront their time in all its moral and linguistic complexity with a vision that is not secondhand. We realise once more, in the 'post-modern' eighties, that just as the adoption of up-to-date modes and technologies is no guarantee of truth, so the use of the oldest ones, painting, drawing, engraving, is no bar to it; one may evade reality either way, or meet it. Those who are drawn to this lovely medium need no longer feel shy, apologetic or defiant about their choice – but neither can they hide behind it. It is a good tool to touch reality with, as good as any other; and the work is all to do, as always.

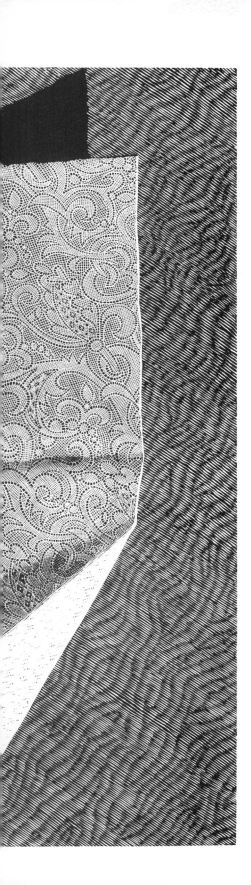

1

The latest renaissance has been spearheaded into the public awareness by Andrew Davidson and Chris Wormell, two young illustrators who have put wood engraving onto the packaging of major retail chains, into the columns of The Times, The Observer and The Sunday Times and into advertising campaigns, as well as into books. Credit for many of these initiatives should go to the design group, Pentagram, which has also commissioned over 200 engravings from Kathleen Lindsley for use as signs on Samuel Webster pubs throughout Yorkshire.

These and other engravers in this first section were born in the 1950s and so are in their early thirties or late twenties. They are still in the process of finding themselves as artists, as one would expect, but the assurance of their work reflects the precocity forced even upon students today, by commerce, in the design field. Engraving is seen as part of graphics. Several who learned engraving (as opposed to being self-taught) learned it on graphic design courses.

Those who work as fine artists, outside the no less commercial gallery circuits, probably have other jobs and develop with less haste. Howard Phipps, who earns his living as a teacher, is one of the few in this generation to make independent prints. He has a painter's eye; his engravings reveal intensity of experience and a still developing sensibility with equal honesty. The rich decisiveness of Harry Brockway's illustration evokes his main profession of sculptor and stonemason; remembering Gertrude Hermes, this seems a particularly profitable background for an engraver. Every piece of his is charged with a remarkable vision and feeling.

Almost all this work, including Phipps' – the dramatic, intelligent illustrations of Jane Lydbury, the delicate craftsmanship of Anthony Christmas – tends to respect the finesse and small size of wood engraving and to partake of a crisp, contemporary, graphic precision. The artists are aware that each mark must be good enough to take enlargement if need be and that if this happens small size must not be seen to have equalled timidity or the lack of a sense of scale.

a

b

c

d

HARRY BROCKWAY, b. 1958, studied sculpture at Kingston (B.A.) and further at
the Royal Academy Schools, where he learned wood engraving with Sarah van
Niekerk. He has also trained as a stone mason. He has exhibited at the Borlase
Gallery, Blewbury, Christ's Hospital Arts Centre and the Trinity Arts Centre,
Tunbridge Wells. Several of the engravings here shown are from *The Lad
Philisides*, a selection of songs, eclogues and elegies from the Countess of
Pembroke's Arcadia, by Sir Philip Sidney (Old Stile Press 1987).

e

f

g

h

a

SUE SCULLARD, b. 1958, was taught to engrave by Yvonne Skargon at the Royal College. She works as a freelance illustrator in various media, using water-colour particularly for topographical or children's books, and engraving for commissioned book illustrations, packaging and advertising work. She has illustrated *The Bride of Lammermuir* for the Folio Society and has contributed to their *Canterbury Tales*. She enjoys engraving decorative subjects and landscape, particularly mountainous scenes, and works on linoleum and vinyl when deadlines are urgent or bolder effects are required.

b

c

ANDREW DAVIDSON, b. 1958, was introduced to wood engraving by Fred Dubery, Yvonne Skargon and John Lawrence at the Royal College. His three years on a graphic design course there, a taste for engraving, the combination of the two in The Lion and Unicorn Press *From the Sea to the Land* and connections with designers have led to a career as a freelance illustrator in which his engravings have been used for Crabtree and Evelyn packaging, Bull's Blood advertising, Sunday Times editorial pages and in *The Iron Man* by Ted Hughes (Faber and Faber).

a

ROSALIND ATKINS, b. 1957, was a student of Tate Adams at the Royal Melbourne Institute of Technology. She works, in Melbourne, mainly as a wood engraver and book illustrator and is currently working for Adams' Lyrebird Press and for the Brindabella Press in conjunction with two of Australia's leading poets. These two engravings are from her own book *Recollections,* published by Lyrebird.

b

a

c

b

CHRISTOPHER WORMELL, b. 1955, worked for nine years in various temporary and part-time jobs while concentrating on painting, without benefit of art school (his father, head of painting at Hornsey, had told him to go to art school if he knew what he wanted to get out of it). He took up wood engraving in 1982 and since 1983 has worked as a full-time illustrator with commissions from, among others, Faber, Penguin and Jonathan Cape, The Radio Times, The Observer, The Times, Goldcrest Films, David Putnam, Saatchi and Saatchi and The Victoria and Albert Museum.

d

e

f

a

b

c

HOWARD PHIPPS, b. 1954, studied painting and printmaking at the Gloucester-
shire College of Art 1971–5, followed by a further year at Brighton. He has made
wood engravings for a number of illustrated books, notably his own purely
visual *Interiors*, for the Whittington Press 1985. A colour print from this won the
Christies' Contemporary Print Award at the 1985 Royal Academy Summer
Exhibition. Howard Phipps has been a member of the Royal West of England
Academy since 1979. He currently lives in Salisbury.

d

f

JANE LYDBURY, b. 1953, originally studied English at Cambridge and taught for some years before turning to art and graphic design. She graduated in 1981 from Camberwell, where she had studied wood engraving under John Lawrence. She lives in London and works as a freelance illustrator. Many of her commissions are executed as wood engravings or as vinyl' or linocuts. The three shown here are from *This Solid Globe*, a book about Shakespeare's theatre, published by the Camberwell Press in 1984.

a

b

c

ANTHONY CHRISTMAS, b. 1953, studied graphic design and is self-taught as an engraver. He has practised as a printmaker since leaving college, fulfilling private commissions and holding exhibitions. Resident in the north of Scotland for ten years, he moved to Derbyshire in 1986 and established the Hermit Press for the production of fine limited edition books illustrated with wood engravings.

d

e

f

g

a   b

c

Jonathan Gibbs, b. 1953, is a painter. Engraving complements that work, as an evening occupation, originally suggested by cutting or carving literally into the surface of chalk drawings done on heavy-duty paper. He has always retained a strong interest in sculpture and in craft processes; engraving satisfies those concerns and provides an outlet for graphic themes in contrast to the predominantly abstract character of his paintings.

Simon King, b. 1951, studied fine art and then printmaking at the Central, learning engraving from Blair Hughes-Stanton and Ian Mortimer. He lives in Cumbria as a painter, printmaker, typographer and bookbinder. He makes large colour linocuts and hand-printed books illustrated with engravings. The two shown here are commissioned work.

a

b

a

b

c

d

KATHLEEN LINDSLEY, b. 1951, educated in Australia, Singapore and England, graduated in fine art from Newcastle, where Leo Wyatt first introduced her to engraving. She has been self-taught thereafter and now lives on the Isle of Skye, where she founded the Struan Craft Workshop in 1979. She works primarily as a wood engraver and illustrator and has had several one-man exhibitions. She describes the Pentagram Samuel Webster commission as providing a great boost to technique – as well as making her work more widely known.

f–i

e

j

k

l

2

Compared to the crisply graphic white-line in section one, those of us in our forties present a diversity of approaches, from cool, tonal composition (Claire Dalby) to robustly physical cutting (Pauline Clark or Gerard Brender à Brandis) which treats the wood as an almost malleable substance. Ray Hedger emphasises the hard, flat printing surface as a mesh of black-line facsimile, with textural infill. Claire Dalby lowers that printing surface itself as Bewick did, to achieve exquisite atmospheric greys. Her vision and technique are classic. Contrasts no less surprising could be made between Anne Jope's meditations, Colin Paynton's mesmeric patterns, which spread across the page like slow explosions, and the vignettes of Ian Stephens, in which the line from Bewick is at its most authentic.

Equally different to the foregoing is the way my contemporaries go about things, their ambitions, the sort of artists they are trying to be.

Ours was the last generation in which engraving was taught as part of an artist's general education. From the late 1960s, art education was completely overhauled and tuition in engraving disappeared for some years. It was resumed under the wing of graphic design – as education with a direct, commercial application. With the exception of Robert Tilleard (self-taught, late '70s) there appears to be no one to bridge the gap.

The former variety of teaching, the sense of isolation occasioned by the break, the concentration of engraving in the graphics departments of fewer schools, with all the shifts of attitude involved therein, may largely explain the noticeable difference in generations between diversity and concentration on technical finesse; but also, whatever work we have done, in our forties we begin to understand where we want to go; we distinguish the influence of teachers and the limitations of fashion and demand, from our own purposes. As I try to reconcile visual experience in its painterly tone with emotionally experienced ideas and destinies, that, at least, is how it seems to me. Edwina Ellis and Peter Smith, latecomers to engraving, bring such emerging certainty to technically inventive and thematically very original work. For Hilary Paynter the state of man is not too grand a theme.

a

b

ROBERT TILLEARD, b. 1949, was trained at Canterbury, Bristol and Brighton Art Colleges and is self-taught as an engraver. He lives and works near Tisbury, Wiltshire, as a painter, etcher and engraver and describes himself as a Wilts', Dorset' and Tuscaniophile.

c

d

e

a

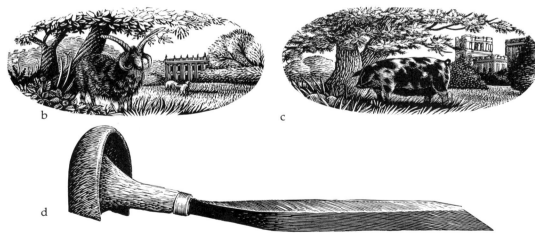

b   c

d

EDWINA ELLIS, b.1946, was originally a jeweller in Sydney, Australia. Wood engraving evolved from learning metal engraving at Sir John Cass College, after settling in London in 1972, and with the help of two summer schools with Simon Brett; colour engraving developed after a visit to Morocco in 1984. Hope, Charity and Prudence are each one of three colour blocks cut for these designs, here reproduced in black; Faith, in full colour, is on the cover. In 1986, Edwina Ellis published a boxed set of five prints from *The Maxims of the Duc de la Rochefoucauld* (see title page).

e

f

g

h

a

b

PETER SMITH, b. 1946, is a painter and printmaker who, since 1983, has been Head of Art and Design at Kingston College of Further Education. From 1977–79 he was West Midlands Fine Art Fellow and has exhibited in the Midlands, London and overseas. He has come to engraving only recently, bringing to it a vision as personal and rooted in experience as it is characteristically low-key.

c

d

e

a

COLIN PAYNTON, b. 1946, lives in Wales and is a watercolour painter and printmaker, self-taught as a wood engraver. He has illustrated several books, notably for the Gregynog Press in Wales, but also for the Gruffyground and Barbarian Presses. A Fellow of the Royal Society of Painter-Etchers and Engravers, he also belongs to various associations of wildlife artists: this is an area both traditional and traditionally limiting for wood engravers and it is exciting to see its conventions so thrillingly transcended.

b

c

a

ANNE JOPE, b. 1945, studied painting at the Central School and did a post–graduate printmaking diploma there; she learned wood engraving from Blair Hughes-Stanton and Ian Mortimer. Turning to painting and thence print-making late, as a mature student, she has exhibited widely in Britain and abroad and describes herself as 'just someone now trying to print in a painterly way, in an effort to understand the inner and outer worlds.'

a

PAULINE CLARK, b.1944, was taught engraving by Mary Maddick (little heard of as an engraver but influential as a teacher) at Luton and has worked in stage design and, since 1969, in picture restoration. Her engraving often reflects the theatre, particularly in an ongoing series of some twenty-eight *Portraits from Opera*, destined for publication with texts by the singers.

b

a

RAY HEDGER, b. 1944. Introduced to engraving by Kenneth Lindley at Swindon School of Art, Ray Hedger's interest was developed by Hermes, Hughes-Stanton and Barrett at the Central School. Later he became interested in film-making as an extension of painting, and was self-taught in this, though in contact with Norman McLaren; his film based on Ted Hughes' *Crow,* begun on a South West Arts grant, went on to win a Gold Seal at the IAC London International Film Festival. Since 1983 he has worked in Community Arts development in Thamesdown and, currently, at RAF Fairford.

b

c

The engravings on this page are reduced by 69%.
The detail opposite is reproduced full size.

a

b

CLAIRE DALBY, b. 1944, learned the rudiments of engraving at the City and Guilds School, where she also specialised in lettering, but never saw anyone else engrave wood until quite recently. Since 1967, she has worked as a wood engraver, watercolour painter and botanical illustrator. She exhibits regularly and her published work includes, among other botanical illustrations, those in *The Observer's Book of Lichens* and two Natural History Museum wallcharts on the subject. In the distinguished Gruffyground Press poetry series, she has engraved a frontispiece for Freda Downie's *Even the Flowers*.

c

d

a

SIMON BRETT, b. 1943, spent several years trying to be a painter in New Mexico and Provence before settling to teaching, in Wiltshire, in 1971. Until 1980, his work as an engraver was largely ephemeral – a monograph on his bookplates was published in 1982 – but since then he has illustrated several books, publishes some of them under the Paulinus Press imprint, and won a Francis Williams Illustration Award with the first, *The Animals of Saint Gregory*. As for others who took to engraving just before 'the break' it was not a commercial prospect – which raised the question 'What is it?'

b

c

a

HILARY PAYNTER, b. 1943, has enjoyed parallel but quite separate careers in education and in engraving for twenty years; she was taught engraving at Portsmouth by Gerry Tucker, another unsung but influential figure. Recently, she has become deeply involved in the renaissance and organisation of the Society of Wood Engravers. She is intrigued, according to mood, by a wide range of subjects – social issues, weathered stones, the state of man – and is prepared to explore these topics in her engravings, often working on several unrelated blocks at any one time.

a

GERARD BRENDER À BRANDIS, b. 1942, of Carlisle, Ontario, calls himself a 'bookwright': as engraver, printer, binder and on occasion papermaker, he has produced about fifteen hand-made, limited edition books since 1969, 'along with a raft of single-leaf prints for framing and lots of ephemera'. He is mostly self-taught as an engraver with some help from Rosemary Kilbourn, and fell in love with the medium on first acquaintance for its clarity, its decisiveness, the movement from dark to light and the wood itself.

b

c

a

b

IAN STEPHENS, b. 1940, has been engraving, on a largely part-time basis, since leaving art school in 1961, fitting it into spare moments of escape from full-time jobs, first as an art teacher in Northampton and more recently as design manager for a large mail-order publishing company. A constant theme is landscape, the natural world and man's place in it and influence upon it. Commissions for bookplates, advertising and editorial illustration have been carried out, but the majority of his work is at a more personal level of expression.

c

d

e

3

Since none was born later than 1937, the artists in this third section are all in their fifties, and turning fifty with a body of work behind you (let alone 'the shock of becoming a grandparent' – John Lawrence on his *Good Babies, Bad Babies*, p. 81) deserves a celebration. A magnificent volume of *Selected Wood Engravings* by John Lawrence was published by the Camberwell Press in 1986. Over the winter of 1985–6, both George Tute and Richard Shirley Smith had major retrospective exhibitions, at the Bristol Museum and the Ashmolean Museum, Oxford, respectively. And Peter Forster took early retirement – making sure there would be a body of work before him, too. For even if life has allowed you to get enough done for a retrospective exhibition, reflection upon the distance travelled at fifty is a girding of the loins for even more fruitful voyaging yet to come. We trust. The engravers in this section and the next are the peak of their powers.

Peter Forster has only recently emerged from the shadows of English Heritage, where they have been hiding his light under their bushel; somehow he appears as a 'new' engraver, when he has been at it for years Born again, perhaps. With John Lawrence, he provides the thing too often missing in engraving, humour. Much of his best work is in colour.

All these engravers have found themselves as artists and have established a level of creativity and a modus vivendi. They were old enough to survive the 'break' by being already launched into work and working contacts. If teaching, they had, before too long, acquired enough influence to ensure that engraving was resumed in schools eventually; the young men and women in section one have been their students.

If there is a leitmotif to their work it is the opposite of the controlled white-line of the younger artists. Many of these engravers are characterised by the free, black-line facsimile cutting, already seen in the work of Ray Hedger (p. 48). There, it derived from the late Kenneth Lindley; in Pat Jaffé's work, homage is paid to Leonard Baskin.

Black-line facsimile cutting means the translation of apparently overlaid drawn pen lines into the smooth, unlayered surface of the block, by cutting *between* the strokes of the drawing, or outside them; and it touches the paradox and fascination of relief printing: that where in painting or drawing, you read a series of marks made, over a period of time, beside or on top of each other on a field which is usually the whole page, in a print a complicated design, apparently of many lines but in fact a single smooth surface, is stamped at one go onto the page, and you usually read within the stamped area alone. The graver draws in white: that's positive; and the wood prints from the black beside where the graver cut: that's positive too. Cut and print are both direct marks, and they are not the same. In the history of modern art, which is the rescue of gesture from illusion, this is a uniquely clear state of affairs.

A second motif is the consciously rich variation of textural marks which patterns 'between' the 'drawn' lines but actually brings them into being. From these textures the mysterious worlds of George Tute and Betty Pennell are evoked, the jollity of John Lawrence's is patterned forth and the work of David Gentleman, Sarah van Niekerk or Miriam Macgregor each draws its separate identity.

Together, these motifs constitute one of the most liberating approaches of the century, which gives to the work of artists of the post-war period an entirely different character to those of the well-documented generations that flourished between the wars; and which is seldom recognised as such. Clearly it applies to the work of many other artists than the handful here represented as well as to others in other sections of this book. Differently expressed, the sparkling cutting of these artists involves the rediscovery and enlargement of nineteenth century reproductive engraving; but where that was microscopic and based in painterly tone, this is vigorously large and exposed in graphic marks – the merely reproductive made creative.

Richard Shirley Smith shares this textural language but makes quite different use of it; the black of the block, which remains in evidence in others' work as recipient of their cutting, is spirited away and the pecked, coruscating textures refer as much to the worn and enduring surfaces of things as to the play of light upon them. In other words, it is to the content and atmosphere of the artist's vision that we are immediately introduced and which in the end we remember, in his and every other case, because that is what artistic maturity gives. In Richard's retrospective, engraving played a major part, but only a part, in an oeuvre that includes painting, collage and elaborate mural decoration; his engraving is largely confined to book work. George Tute, on the other hand, has made large, independent, wood engraved prints, up to 16″ × 12″ in size – which is colossal for this medium. The title of his equally impressive exhibition simply said 'George Tute – Wood Engraver'. It is enough.

a

b

c

d

CORDELIA JONES, b. 1936, discovered engraving through contact with Patricia Jaffé at Cambridge. As a writer of books for older children, it appealed to her as the perfect complement to type; the first book she illustrated was her own *A Cat Called Camouflage* (1970). Dissatisfied with the printing of the engravings, she bought a press in 1977 and began to produce cards, letterheads and other ephemera. In 1984 she exhibited in *The Artist at Work,* at Norwich, and in 1986 illustrated two books for the Japanese publishers, Iwanami Shoten.

a

b

c

ROSALIND BLISS, b. 1937 in London, was educated in Scotland and took her diploma at Edinburgh College of Art in mural painting. She lives in London as a painter, a painter of screens and a part-time teacher and took up engraving as recently as 1971. Her engravings are done mostly for pleasure, though she also does bookplates, letterheadings and Christmas cards on commission.

d

e

f

a

YVONNE ELSTON, b. 1935, is an artist in black-and-white media, drawings and prints, who has exhibited widely over the years, particularly in international print exhibitions in Europe. Drawing is her main field. In engraving, to which she was originally introduced by Gerry Tucker, her preoccupation is with textural and tonal variations and the 'colour' that may be achieved by the balance of blacks and whites and greys.

b

a

b

MIRIAM MACGREGOR, b. 1935, worked for the publishers B. T. Batsford for several years in their Art Department and subsequently freelance. In 1977 she joined the Whittington Press, where she still works as a part-time compositor, and for whom she has illustrated a distinguished and delightful sequence of books, as well as others, for other fine presses or publishers for whom Whittington prints. No one taught her to engrave: Stanley Lawrence gave her a demonstration over the counter, she says.

c

d

e

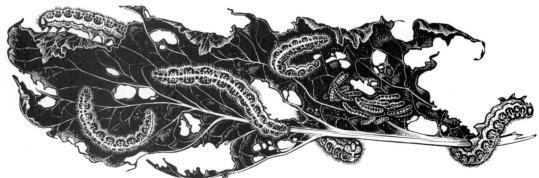

f

a

b

c

PATRICIA JAFFÉ, b. 1935, trained as an academic and has constantly looked upon painting and printmaking as an escape. She remains an amateur wood engraver in her own estimation, but is still looking for time to do more. Her subjects tend to be single, isolated and small, or else pay homage to draughtsmen who lived too early to be able to design for wood engravers. Patricia Jaffé learned to engrave from books and then learned to make wood-cuts from Leonard Baskin, for whom she subsequently worked as studio assistant 1959–62. She exhibits under the name of Milne Henderson.

d

e

f

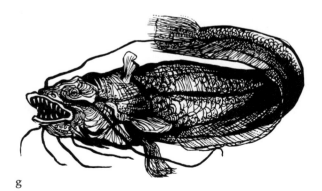

g

RICHARD SHIRLEY SMITH, b. 1935, first achieved prominence as a wood engraver – he has illustrated over thirty books, among them *The Poems of Percy Bysshe Shelley* for the Limited Editions Club, *Messer Pietro Mio* (Libanus Press) and others for the Folio Society – but he now also works as a painter and maker of mural decorations. Some of his finest independent works have been done in collage, his use of which is as individual and perfectionist as his engraving. He has also made many bookplates and ephemera and was entirely self-taught as an engraver.

g

PETER FORSTER, b. 1934, went to two art schools one after the other and learned wood engraving from Mary Maddick at the first. After twenty-one years, four months and twenty-six days as a graphic designer in the Civil Service, he became a full-time engraver on May Day 1985. In 1987 he was the subject of a film on BBC2's Saturday Review. He works, to Wagner and weak tea, in the patriotic-satirical mode and his *New Temple of British Worthies*, in the heroick-satirical mode, is ongoing, in colour.

e

f

g

h

i

j

k.

SARAH VAN NIEKERK, b. 1934, learned engraving from Gertrude Hermes at the
Central School and was later herself tutor in wood engraving at the Royal
Academy Schools from 1976–86. She is a Fellow of the Royal Society of Painter-
Etchers and Engravers, The Printmakers Council and The Art Workers Guild
and has exhibited regularly and all over the world. Though Sarah van Niekerk
has illustrated several books, for example for the Folio Society and the Gregynog
Press, she is primarily a maker of independent prints – wood engravings and
large colour wood' and lino cuts.

a

MICHAEL RENTON, b. 1934, designer and lettering craftsmen, learned his engraving as an apprentice 'in the trade' (what was left of it). This was more by luck than judgement and gave him a sense of the block as firstly a printable object, as well as some habits he has had to try to overcome. He likes each cut to be expressive as a cut, not simply as part of an effect. He lives in East Sussex, exhibits regularly in the area and was much involved with the Eric Gill centenary; his introduction to *The Engraved Bookplates of Eric Gill* (1987) is a model of practical insight.

b

c

d

e

f

a

b

c

d

JOHN LAWRENCE, b. 1933, is one of the country's most prolific and most appealing illustrators, in a variety of media. He learned his engraving from Gertrude Hermes at an evening class at the Central and all the engraving he has done has grown out of his book illustration or ephemeral commissions – with spectacular exceptions like *Rabbit and Pork: Rhyming Talk* which was his own idea. He aims to achieve a richness of texture and a fairly free engraving style, and prefers to be lighthearted where he can.

e

a

GEORGE TUTE, b. 1933, another of Gertrude Hermes' students, was Principal Lecturer in Graphic Design at Bristol 1962–87 while simultaneously pursuing a busy career of exhibitions and commissions as painter, illustrator and wood engraver. He was also the first chairman of the resurrected Society of Wood Engravers. Within its apparently narrow restrictions of material and technique, he finds engraving capable of infinitesimal variations of expression and style, limited only by the imagination of the artist; its potential has still to be shown, although the best examples of the past will take some beating.

b–d

a

SHIRLEY MUNGAPEN, b. 1933, painter, engraver and writer, has worked as an art
therapist for many years and became a lay pastor in 1983. She was one of Gerry
Tucker's students at Portsmouth. She sees artists' lives as being enriched by
their visual experience and believes they sometimes have their fingers on the
pulse of humanity. In wood engraving, these visual experiences, allied to a
standard of craftsmanship, offer a balance of the practical and the inspirational
in which she is happy to be involved.

b

c

d

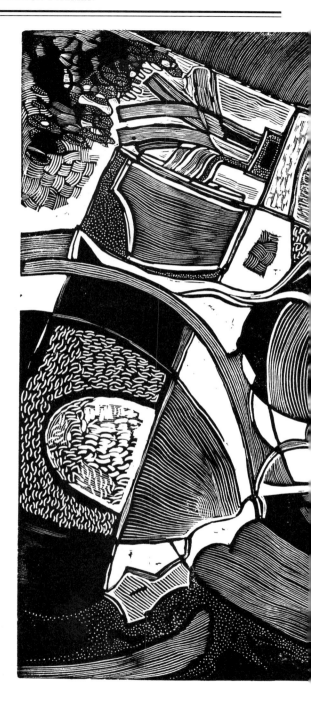

GARRICK PALMER, b. 1933, retired from teaching at Winchester School of Art in 1986 and is now working full-time at illustration, engraving and photography. Several books illustrated by him have been published by the Folio Society and The Imprint Society of Massachusetts.

a

YVONNE SKARGON, b. 1931, works mainly as a book illustrator. Watercolours, drawings and wood engravings, often on botanical and culinary themes, have been commissioned by many leading English publishers. For many years she worked as a typographer and book designer and for five years taught wood engraving at the Royal College. She herself studied wood engraving with Blair Hughes-Stanton and John O'Connor at Colchester. She now lives mainly in Suffolk where her botanical and naturalist interests find expression both in her work and in gardening.

b

c

a

b

DAVID GENTLEMAN, b. 1930, one of the few illustrators to achieve star billing (*David Gentleman's Britain*, 1982, *David Gentleman's London*, 1985) feels the conventional divide between painting and graphic design to be more academic than real. He was first inspired as an engraver by Bewick and Ravilious and studied under John Nash and Reynolds Stone at the Royal College. In work which ranges from postage stamps (1962 onwards) to the platform-length murals at Charing Cross Underground Station he has influentially taken engraving off the printed page, as well as using it in books, covers and advertising. All his engraving has been commissioned.

c

d

a

BETTY PENNELL, b. 1930, was at the Royal College from 1949–52 and learned engraving from John Nash and Edward Bawden. From 1959–64 she taught at Birmingham College of Art and since then has had her own studio as a painter and engraver in Herefordshire. As a painter, she uses engraving as an alternative means to express her feeling for English gardens and the countryside. She began engraving on wood and metal but now works on plastics of various kinds.

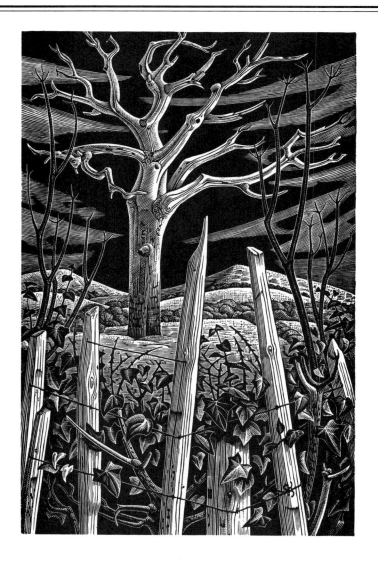

4

The distinction between generations seems to break down. Monica Poole's print is Winter, but the fourth season of an artist's life, God willing, is Indian summer. If Frank Martin does less engraving now, it is simply because he is busy with other things and his interests have moved on; the quality of his engraved work and his support for the medium remain an inspiration. Peter Reddick, who was Gregynog Arts Fellow in 1979–80, is one of the best examples of the approach to engraving described in the previous section; Reg Boulton, in the large and spectacular engravings he makes on plastic – too large for this book – is another.

To separate these four from the previous group when some belong there stylistically and all are together reaping the harvest of fifty-plus years, is to recognise not just a further ten or fifteen year difference in age, but the difference in numbers too and the significance of the gap between: these are facts of history. Anyone born between Peter Reddick (1924) and David Gentleman (1930) who might have been an engraver, wasn't. To be adult or grow up straight into a major war is a profoundly different experience from growing up during or after it. And the second major hiatus in engraving, the withdrawal of teaching (that is, of confidence in a future) occurred as they approached fifty. There were no celebrations but only, apparently, a closing-down.

The achievement of these four and their contemporaries is, in that context, the more remarkable, but especially that of Monica Poole.

Almost alone among the artists in this book, she has kept faith with wood engraving as the independent, original print. Though, as a younger woman, she did her share of illustrational work, she has concentrated more and more exclusively on a visual art which does not illustrate another, verbal idea, but which tells its own truth. Of course, many engravers – Hilary Paynter, Betty Pennell, Sarah van Niekerk, too many to list – make independent prints, but most are involved in illustration too, for employment and to make their reputations. And, of course, engraving is ideally suited, it is part of its history, to appear as the handmaiden of literature. Monica Poole has chosen otherwise, to be the mistress of her own vision, to risk the less frequent exposure and insecure rewards of exhibitions and to rest her case, classically, on her art, as an engraver on wood. It is a singular and radiant example.

a

b

PETER REDDICK, b. 1924, works as a book illustrator, mainly using wood engravings. He also takes on work for advertising, occasionally. He has illustrated books for the Folio Society, the Gregynog Press, Collins, Dorling Kindersley, The Limited Editions Club of New York and The Readers Digest and his other fields of work include watercolours and colour woodcuts. He exhibits with the Royal Society of Painter Etchers and the Royal West of England Academy.

c

d

a

b

REG BOULTON, b. 1924, trained as a teacher, after service in the R.A.F. and taught art at Huntingdon Grammar School for ten years, engraving illustrations for the Vine Press meanwhile. For eighteen years he taught at Colleges of Education in Yorkshire and Hereford and returned to engraving on early retirement. He is mainly interested in design problems and especially likes working with books and with type or lettering. He cuts lettering in slate and engraves in metal. He has also been active in organising national and international exhibitions of wood engraving.

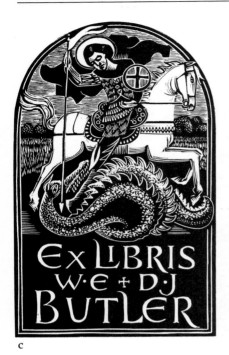

c

d

e

f

a

MONICA POOLE, b. 1921, studied with John Farleigh on the Book Production course at the Central School 1946–49. Her own book on *The Wood Engravings of John Farleigh* was published in 1985, while *Monica Poole – Wood Engraver*, with a text by George Mackley, appeared in 1984. Her list of exhibitions contains many contributions to shows of engraving and on botanical themes, in Europe and in the U.S.A. She tends to engrave rather stark subjects at one time and gentler landscapes at another; on the whole she is more interested in the former.

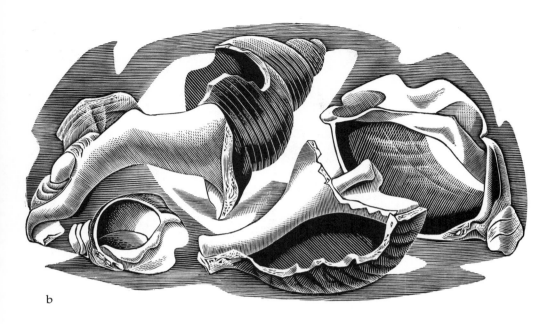

b

c

a

b

FRANK MARTIN, b. 1921, studied with Gertrude Hermes at St. Martin's. Between 1948 and 1966 he worked as a freelance illustrator and wood engraver, for numerous book and magazine publishers, advertisers and private clients. Since 1966, he has been primarily a printmaker in woodcut, etching and drypoint. Between 1953 and 1980 he taught engraving and etching at Camberwell, from 1976 as Head of Graphic Arts. He has had sixteen one-man exhibitions, in the U.K. and abroad, since 1956.

c

d

e

f

Born 1902

Born 1912

Born 1912

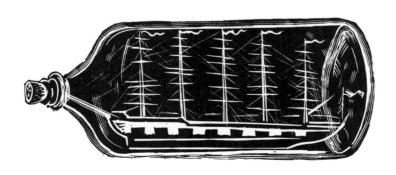

RICHARD SHIRLEY SMITH 72

a from *The Poems of Shelley*
b–f from *Messer Pietro Mio*
g from *Buzz-buzz* (Gruffyground Press)

Head of a girl from Vines   page 60

YVONNE SKARGON 88

a July Garden, 1984
b March, Suffolk, 1984
c November Sky, 1984

PETER SMITH 40

a Douglas, 1986
b Working late, 1986
c Underground, 1986
d Baptism, 1984
e Mr. Punch, 1987

IAN STEPHENS 58

a Mute Swan, 1981
b Snowstorm, 1986
c Cottesbrooke, 1983
d Near Bradden, 1985
e Winter Wood, 1982

SYBELLA STYLES 109

ROBERT TILLEARD 36

a Chisenbury Priory, Wilts, 1987
b Butlers Cottage, Wilts, 1985
c Long Hall, Wilts, 1985
d Ropley Grove, Hampshire, 1986
e Pythouse Farm, Tisbury, 1984

GEORGE TUTE 82

a Norwegian Folk Story, (Time and Life),
  1986
b–d Three engravings from *Under the
  Hawthorn*, (Dent), 1981

CHRISTOPHER WORMELL 22

a Two Gloucester Old Spots, 1984,
  Observer Magazine
b *A Quiet Life* (Beryl Bainbridge) cover
  design
c Peacock, 1985, The Times
d Foxhunt, for *English Country Traditions*
  by Ian Niail, Victoria and Albert
e Wheatfield, for Tesco bran flakes
  package, 1986
f Potter Heigham Church, 1985, for V. & A.
  headed notepaper

Field of Oats (Observer Magazine)
page 12

Rosalind Atkins, 73 Fenwick Street, Clifton Hill, Victoria 3068, Australia

John Biggs, 68 Stanford Avenue, Brighton, Sussex, BN1 6FD   0273 554790

Rosalind Bliss, 149 Notting Hill Gate, London W11   01 727 5406

Reg Boulton, 30 Broomy Hill, Hereford HR4 0LH   0432 266910

Gerard Brender a Brandis, 1459 Progreston Road North, Carlisle, Ontario, Canada L0R 1H0

Simon Brett, 12 Blewhorn Street, Marlborough, Wilts SN8 1BT 0672 52905

Harry Brockway, Leur Remm, 3 Lower New Road, Cheddar, Somerset.

Anthony Christmas, 15 Robertson Road, Buxton, Derbyshire SK17 9DY

Pauline Clark, 32 St. Martins Avenue, Luton, Beds. LU2 7LQ   0582 411103

Claire Dalby, 132 Gordon Road, Camberley, Surrey, GU15 2JQ   0276 21230

Andrew Davidson, 24 Gwydyr Road, Shortlands, Bromley BR2 0EX   01 466 6072

E.N. Ellis, 4 Queensberry Mews West, London SW7 2DU   01 589 6417

Yvonne Elston, 7 Devonshire Avenue, Southsea, Hants P04 9EA

Peter Forster, 30 Wilberforce Road, London N4 2SW   01 226 1336

David Gentleman, 25 Gloucester Crescent, London NW1 7DL   01 485 8824

Jonathan Gibbs, 4 Epworth Terrace, Amberley, Stroud, Glos. GL5 5AJ   045387 3500

Ray Hedger, Cam House, High Street, Fairford, Glos. GL7 4AD   0285 713082

Patricia Jaffé, Grove Lodge, Trumpington Street, Cambridge CB2 1QG

Cordelia Jones, 1 The Crescent, Cromer, Norfolk NR27 9EX   0263 514269

Anne Jope, Kew Cottage, Lambridge Lane, Badgemore, Henley-on-Thames, Oxon. RG9 4NR   0491 576531

Simon King, Ashton House, Beetham, Cumbria LA7 7AL   044 82 2194

John Lawrence, 22a Castlewood Road, London N16 6DW   01 809 3482

Kathleen Lindsley, Struan Craft Workshop, Struan, Isle of Skye IV56 8FE   047072 284

Jane Lydbury, 14 Fingal Street, London SE10 0JJ   01 853 4431

Miriam Macgregor, 30 Whittington Village, Cheltenham, GL54 4HD   0242 820892

Frank Martin, 55 St. Mary's Grove, London W4 3LW   01 747 3686

Enid Marx, 39 Thornhill Road, Barnsbury Square, London N1 1JS   01 607 2286

Shirley Mungapan, Sunnyside, Ashlett Road, Fawley, Southampton SO4 1DS   0703 898250

Garrick Palmer, 8 Firs Avenue, Cowplain, nr. Portsmouth, Hants. PO8 8RS   0705 252894

Hilary Paynter, 19 Montague Road, Richmond, Surrey, TW10 6QW   01 940 3553

Colin Paynton, Oerle Hall, Berriew, Powys, Wales SY21 8QX   068 687 531

Betty Pennell, Lower Bibbletts, Hoarwithy, Hereford HR2 6QF   043 270324

Howard Phipps, 53 Ravenscroft, Salisbury, Wilts SP2 8DL   0722 21726

Monica Poole, 67 Hadlow Road, Tonbridge, Kent TN9 1QB   0732 353806

William Rawlinson, 10 Myatt's Field, Harvington, Evesham WR11 5NG   0386 870469

Peter Reddick, 18 Hartington Park, Bristol BS6 7ES   0272 49167

Michael Renton, Brook Granary, Icklesham, Winchelsea, East Sussex TN36 4AX   0424 814535

Sue Scullard, 52 Mount Pleasant, Paddock Wood, Tonbridge, Kent   089 283 6301

Richard Shirley Smith, 9 Douro Place, London W8 5PH   01 937 9674

Yvonne Skargon, 44 Prentice Street, Lavenham, Suffolk   0787 247748

Peter Smith, 36 Bicester Road, Richmond, Surrey TW9 4QN   01 878 3078

Ian Stephens, 46 Yardley Drive, Northampton NN2 8PE   0604 842399

Sybella Stiles, Brooklands Bar, Ripe, Lewes, East Sussex BN8 6AR 032183 423

Robert Tilleard, Pythouse Farm, Tisbury, Salisbury, Wilts.   0747 870801

George Tute, 46 Eastfield, Wetbury on Trym, Bristol BS9 4BE   0272 624631

Sarah van Niekerk*, Wilcote Grange, Finstock, Oxon. OX7 3EA   099 386 354

Christopher Wormell, 61 Russell Road, London N13 4RS   01 881 5823

all artists in this handbook
may be contacted through
the Society of Wood Engravers:
secretary: Hilary Paynter
P.O. Box 355, Richmond, Surrey TW10 6LE